Learn Legal Terminology in 2015

Essential English-Chinese **Legal** Terms

英语—中文

中文—英语

José Luis Leyva - Wei Wong

PREFACE

A new year is always a great opportunity to learn. A few minutes every day will help in your goal for personal and professional improvement. Being bilingual is an asset; and mastering different fields of speciality will make a difference in your bilingual skills. This book can be a helpful resource to learn the essential English-Chinese LEGAL terms. Learn 4 to 5 terms each day and at the end of 2015 you will master the essential LEGAL terminology in this language combination. This book contains only the most frequently used LEGAL terminology in English and Chinese.

ENGLISH-CHINESE

英语—中文

A

Abandonment, 遗弃/放纵

Abate, 缓和/消除

Abet, 教唆/怂恿

Abide by, 遵守/履行

Abortion, 流产/堕胎

Above-named, 上述的

Abscond, 潜逃/逃匿

Absconder, 潜逃者

Abstract, 摘要/抽象的/提取

Abuse, 滥用/诽谤

Abuse of discretion, 自由裁量权的滥用

Abuser, 滥用者

Access, 通道/接近

Accessory, 配件/同谋

Accommodation (in case of disability), 膳宿（在残疾的情况下）

Accomplice, 共犯

According to, 按照

Accounting, 会计

Accounting books, 会计账簿

Accrue/accruing, 累积/累计

Accusation, 指控

Accusatory instrument, 控告起诉书

Accuse, 指控

Accused, 被告/被指控的

Acknowledge, 承认/告知收到/表示感谢

Acquit, 宣告无罪

Acquittal, 宣告无罪

Act, 法案；行动

Acting in the capacity of, 以...的身份行事

Action, 行动/起诉/作用

Addict, 沉溺/上瘾的

Address, 地址/处理/讲话

Address, 地址/处理/讲话

Address, 地址/处理/讲话

Adjourn, 休庭/延期

Adjournment, 休庭期间/延期

Adjudicate, 判决/宣判

Adjudicating, 判决/宣判

Adjudication, 判决/宣判

Adjustment, 调整/适应

Administer the oath to…, 为…主持宣誓仪式

Admissible, 可接纳的

Admissible evidence, 可接纳的证据

Admission of Service, 送达回执

Admit, 承认/允许

Admit into evidence, 接纳为证据

Admonish, 告诫/提醒

Adolescent, 青少年/青春期的

Adopt, 收养/采纳/批准

Adopt(ed), 被收养的/被采纳的

Adoption, 收养/采纳

Adult Detention Center, 成人拘留中心

Advantage, 优点/好处

Adversarial witness, 对抗性证人

Advice of rights, 建议的权利

Advisement of rights, 权利告诫

Advisory, 建议性的/劝告的

Advocacy, 拥护/支持/鼓吹

Advocate, 拥护/支持/鼓吹

Affidavit, 宣誓书

Affidavit of prejudice, 偏见宣誓书

Affidavit of Service, 送达证明书

Affirm, 确认/肯定

Aforementioned, 前述的

Aforesaid, 上述的

Aftercare, 疾病治疗后的调养

Age, 年龄/时代

Aggravated, 加重的

Aggravating circumstances, 可加重罪行的情况

Aggravating circumstances, 可加重罪行的情况

Aggrieved, 受到侵犯的/（因受伤害）愤愤不平的

Agree, 同意/一致

Agreement, 协议/一致

Agreement, 协议/一致

Aid and abet, 教唆/协谋

Alcohol sensor, 酒精传感器

Alibi, 不在场证据/托辞

Alien, 外国的/陌生的

Alimony, 赡养费（离婚后丈夫给妻子的）

Allegation, 断言/主张/指控

Allege, 断言/主张/指控

Alleged, 声称的/不可靠的

Allocate(d), 分配/分派

Amend, 修订/改进

Amended information, 修改后的信息

Amendment, 修订/改进/修正案

Amount, 数量/总额

Amphetamine, 苯丙胺

Angel dust, 天使粉

Annuity, 年金/养老金

Annul, 废除/宣告无效

Answer, 答辩/答辩状

Appeal, 上诉/吸引力/诉请

Appeal, 上诉/吸引力/诉请

Appear, 出现

Appearance, 出现/外观

Appellant, 上诉人/上诉的

Appellant, 上诉人/上诉的

Appellate Court, 上诉法院

Applicant, 申请人

Application, 申请/应用

Application fee, 申请费

Apply for, 申请

Apply to, 适用于

Appoint, 任命/指定

Approval, 同意/批准

Arbitration, 仲裁/公断

Argue, 主张/辩论

Argument, 辩论/理由/论证

Armed forces, 武装部队

Armed robbery, 持械抢劫

Arraignment, 提讯/传讯/责难

Arrangement, 安排/整理

Arrearage, 迟滞/欠款

Arrears, 拖欠款项/待做的工作

Arrest, 逮捕/拘留/吸引

Arrest record, 逮捕记录

Arrest warrant, 逮捕令/拘票

Arson, 纵火/纵火罪

Arsonist, 纵火犯

Ask for, 请求/要求

Asked and answered, 提问和回答

Assault, 攻击/抨击

Assault, 袭击/抨击

Assault and battery, 殴打/人身攻击

Assault with a deadly weapon, 用致命武器袭击

Assault, aggravated使用暴力威胁的严重罪行

Assessment, 估计/评估

Assets, 资产/优点

Associate justice, 最高法院的陪审法官/助理法官

Associate justice of the Supreme Court, 最高法院的陪审法官

Assume, 假定/担任

Assumption, 假定/担任

At that time, 那个时候

At the request of, 应...的请求

At this time, 此时

Attached, 附加的/依恋的

Attempt, 尝试/努力

Attorney, 律师

Attorney General, 总检察长/司法部长

Attorney General's Office, 总检察长办公室

Authority, 权力/当局/专家

Authorization, 授权/委任状

Auto theft, 盗车罪

Award, 授予/给予/奖金

B

Baby sitting, 保姆

Bail, 保释/保释金/担保人

Bail bond, 保释金

Bail bondsman, 保释担保人

Bail forfeiture, 保释金没收

Bail jumping, 弃保潜逃/保释中逃走

Bail review, 保释审查

Bailiff, 法警/区镇的地方长官

Balance, 平衡/天平/制衡

Ballistics report, 弹道学报告

Bank levy, 银行税

Bank robbery, 抢劫银行

Bank statement, 银行对账单

Bankruptcy, 破产/倒闭

Bar association, 律师协会

Based on, 基于

Basis, 基础/原则

Batter, 猛击/打坏

Battery, 殴打

Battery, spousal, 夫妻间的殴打威胁

Belief, 相信/信念

Bench, 法官

Bench conference, 庭前会议

Bench trial, 法官审理/无陪审员的审判

Bench trial/Court trial, 法官审理/法庭审理

Bench warrant, 法院拘票

Benefits, 利益/保险金

Beyond a reasonable doubt, 超出合理怀疑

Birth certificate, 出生证明

Bizarre behavior, 怪异的行为

Blacken out, 使...熄灭/用...涂掉

Blood alcohol level, 血醇水平

Blood alcohol test, 血液酒精测试

Blow, 吹/殴打

Blue Book, 蓝皮书

Blue Book Value, 蓝皮书值

Board of Pardons, 赦免委员会

Bodily harm, 身体伤害

Body attachment, 连接体

Bond, 结合/债券

Bond requirement, 保证金要求

Bondsman, 保证人

Book, 书/账目/预约

Booking, 预约

Booking number, 预约号

Bound, 划界/界限

Brain death, 脑死亡

Break, 休息/打破

Break the lease, 解除租赁

Breaking and entering, 破门而入

Breath alcohol test, 酒精呼气测试

Breathalyzer, 呼吸测醉器

Bribe, 贿赂

Bribery, 贿赂

Brief, 案件陈述

Bring an action, 提起诉讼

Bring to trial, 审判

Bruise, 伤痕/瘀青

Bulletproof, 防弹

Bulletproof vest, 防弹背心

Burden of proof, 举证责任

Bureau of Labor Statistics, 美国劳工统计局

Burglary, 盗窃

Business like manner, 商业方式

C

Calendar, 日历/日程表

Capital offense, crime, 死罪

Capital punishment, 死刑

Car insurance, 汽车险

Car theft, 盗车

Care, custody and control, 照料、保管和控制

Caregiver, 看护者

Careless driving, 疏忽驾驶

Carelessness, 疏忽

Carjacking, 劫车

Case, 情况/案例

Case number, 案件编号

Case of action, 诉讼案件

Case type, 案件类型

Causation, 因果关系

Cease and desist, 停止

Censorship, 检查（制度）

Certificate, 执照/认可

Certified, 经认证的

Certify, 证实/发证书给

Certify as an adult, 证实为成年人

Certiorari, 诉讼文件移送命令

Chain of custody, 监管链

Challenge, 挑战/质疑

Challenge, 挑战/质疑

Challenge for cause, 有正当理由的反对

Chambers, 室/会所

Change of plea, 请求变更

Change of venue, 移送管辖

Charge, 指控/管理/费用

Charge, 指控/管理/费用

Check off, 核对/扣款

Chemical dependency, 化学药品依赖

Child, 儿童

Child abuse, 虐待儿童

Child Care, 儿童保育

Child Care assistance, 儿童保育协助

Child molestation, 猥亵儿童

Child Support, 子女抚养费

Child's Best Interest, 儿童的最大利益

Children, 儿童

Circumstances, aggravating, 加重罪行的情况

Circumstances, mitigating, 减轻罪行的情况

Circumstantial evidence, 旁证/间接证据

Citation, 引用/传票

Cite, 引用/传讯

City Attorney, 市检察长

Civil action, 民事诉讼

Civil commitment, 民事拘禁令

Civil Law Notary, 民事公证

Civil penalties, 民事处罚

Civil rights, 民事权利

Claim, 请求权/索赔

Clear and convincing evidence, 明确和令人信服的证据

Clear and convincing evidence, 明确和令人信服的证据

Clemency, 仁慈/温和

Clerical, 书记的/事务上的

Clerk, 职员

Closing argument, 结案陈词

Cocaine, 可卡因

Co-defendant, 同案被告

Collateral, 平行的/附属的

Collection agency, 收缴欠款的代理公司

Collection services, 收缴欠款服务

Collector, 收款员

Commission, 委员会/佣金

Commissioner, 专员/委员

Commit, 犯罪/委托/承诺

Commit, 犯罪/委托/承诺

Community Court, 社区法庭

Community service, 社区服务

Commutation, 交换/代偿/减刑

Commute, 通勤/减刑

Companion, 同伴

Compensatory parenting time, 补偿性亲子时间

Competency evaluation, 能力评估

Complainant, 原告

Complaint, 投诉/控告/起诉状

Compliance, 服从/遵守

Comply, 遵从/服从

Composite drawing, 合成制图

Conciliation Court, 调解法庭

Concurrent sentences, 合并判刑

Conditional release, 假释

Conditions, 条件/情况

Conditions of release, 释放条件

Confer, 商谈/授予

Confession, 招供/认错

Confidential, 秘密的/担任机密工作的

Confiscate, 没收/充公

Conflict of interest, 利益冲突

Consecutive sentences, 连续判决

Consent, 同意/准许

Consent, 同意/准许

Consideration, 考虑/关心/对价

Conspicuous, 明显的

Conspiracy, 密谋/共谋

Constitute, 构成/制定

Constitutional right, 宪法权利

Contempt, 轻视/蔑视

Contempt motion, 蔑视动议

Contentious, 好辩的/有争议的

Contest, 争夺/辩驳

Contested case, 有争议的案件

Continuance, 继续

Continue, 继续

Controlled substance, 列管药物

Convict, 证明有罪/宣判有罪

Convict, 证明有罪/宣判有罪

Conviction, 确信/定罪

Coroner, 验尸官

Corpus delicti, 犯罪事实

Costs, 成本/花费

Counsel, 律师/法律顾问/ 劝告

Counsel table, 法律顾问表

Counseling service, 咨询服务

Counselor, 顾问/律师

Count, 计算/视为

Counter motion, 反向动议

Counterclaim, 反诉

County Attorney, 郡检察官

County Attorney's Office, 郡检察官办公室

County jail, 郡看守所

Court, 法庭/法院/院子

Court Administrator, 法院管理员

Court appointed attorney, 法院指定的律师

Court clerk, 书记员

Court File Number, 法院档案编号

Court house, 法庭

Court interpreter, 法院翻译员

Court is adjourned, 休庭

Court officer, 法庭保卫

Court order, 法院指令

Court Record, 法庭记录

Court reporter, 法院书记官

court room, 法庭

Court, District, 法院，区

Court, Juvenile, 法院，少年

Coverage, 新闻报道/涵盖范围

Credit Bureau, 征信社

Creditor, 债权人

Crime, 犯罪/罪行

Crime, 犯罪/罪行

Crime scene, 犯罪现场

Crime wave, 犯罪浪潮

Crimes of moral turpitude, 道德沦丧罪

Criminal history, 犯罪史

Criminal insanity, 犯罪时正患精神病者

Criminal justice stakeholders, 刑事司法权益相关者

Criminal record/history, 犯罪记录/历史

Criminal sexual conduct, 犯罪性行为

Criminal sexual contact, 犯罪性接触

Criteria, 标准/准则

Cross examination, 盘问/交叉询问

Cross-examine, 盘问/交叉询问

Current(ly), 当前的/流行的

Custodial, 监禁的/保管的

Custodial parent, 作为监护人的父母

Custodial/Non-Custodial Parent, 作为监护人/非监护人的父母

Custody, 监护/拘留

D

Damages, 毁坏/损害赔偿（金）

Date of birth, 出生日期

Daycare, 日托

Deadline, 最后期限

Deadly weapon, 致命的武器

Deal, 处理/交易

Death penalty, 死刑

Death Row, 死囚区

Debt, 债务/义务

Debt-holder, 债权人

Debtor, 债务人

Decree, 判决/命令

Deduction, 扣除/推理

Deed, 行为/契约

Default, 违约/默认

Default judgment, 缺席判决

Defendant, 被告

Defense, 辩护/防卫

Defense attorney, 辩护律师

Defer, 推迟/服从

Deferment, 延期

Deferred Income, 递延收益

Deferred prosecution, 迟延起诉

Deferred sentence, 推迟宣判

Defraud, 诈骗

Denial, 否认/拒绝

Deny, 否认/拒绝

Deny a motion, 否决动议

Deny parenting time, 否决亲子时间

Dependence, 依赖/信赖

Dependent, 受供养人

Depending on, 依赖于

Deponent, 证人/提出口供者

Depose, 宣誓作证

Deposition, 证言/宣誓作证

Depriving, 剥夺

Deptartment of Public Safety, 公共安全部

Deputy, 副职/代表

Deputy Court Administrator, 法院副管理员

Detained, 被拘留的/扣押的

Deterrent, 威慑的/制止的

Developmental, 发展的

Direct evidence, 直接证据

Direct examination, 当事人 (辩护人)对己方证人作的初步询问

Disabled, 残障的

Disagreement, 不一致/争论

Disclose, 揭露/公开

Discount, 折扣/低估/不信

Discovery, 发现/发觉/发现物

Discretion, 裁量权/谨慎

Disinterested Third Party, 无利害关系的第三方

Dismiss, 解雇/驳回

Dismiss a charge, 驳回指控

Dismiss a claim, 驳回索赔

Dismiss with prejudice, 有损害驳回起诉(不可以再诉)

Dismiss without prejudice, 无损害驳回起诉(可以再诉)

Dismissal, 免职/驳回/拒绝受理

Dismissed, 驳回的/摒弃的

Disorderly conduct, 扰乱治安行为

Dispatch center, 调度中心

Dispatcher, 调度员/调度器

Dispense with, 摒弃/没有...也行

Disposition, 性格/部署

Disproportionately high costs, 不成比例的高成本

Dispute, 争端/质疑

Dissolution, 解除

District Court, 州地方法院

Disturbing the peace, 扰乱治安

Diversion Program, 分流方案

Divorce, 分离/离婚

DNA sample, DNA样本

Docket, 单据/备审案件目录

Domestic abuse, 家庭暴力

Domestic abuse classes, 家庭暴力级别

Domestic violence, 家庭暴力

Double jeopardy, 一罪两罚

Driving permit, 驾驶执照

Driving record, 驾驶记录

Drop the charge, 放弃指控

Drug abuse, 药物滥用

Drunk driving, 酒后驾车

Due diligence, 应有的注意/尽职调查

Due process, 法定诉讼程序

DUI, 酒后驾车

Duty, 责任/税

DWI/DUI (Driving while intoxicated/Driving while
impaired/Driving under the influence),

酒后驾车（极度兴奋时驾车/能力受损时驾车/酒后驾车）

.

E

Effect, 结果/引起

Egregious, 过分的/惊人的

Electronic home monitoring, 电子家庭监控

Elementary school age, 小学入学年龄

Eligibility, 合格/有资格

Embezzlement, 盗用/侵吞

Employer, 雇主

Employer Identification Number, 雇主识别号码

Endanger, 危及/危害

Endangerment, 危害/受到危害

Endorse, 赞同/背书于

Enforce, 实施/强制执行

Enhanceable offense, 可加强的罪行

Enjoin, 命令/禁止

Enter, 进入/登记

Enter a plea, 为自己辩护

Enter an order, 做出判令

Entertain, 娱乐/招待

Entice, 引诱/诱使

Enticement, 诱人/诱惑

Entrapment, 圈套/俘获

Equal protection, 平等的保护

Equitable/Equal, 公平的/平等的

Establishment, 建立/机构

Estate, 财产/房地产

Estimate, 估计/估价

Evict, 驱逐/依法收回

Eviction, 驱逐/依法收回

Evidence, 证据/迹象

Evidence, circumstantial, 证据，间接的

Evidence, direct, 证据，直接的

Evidentiary hearing, 证据听证会

Examination, direct, 询问，直接的

Exclusionary rule, 证据排除规则

Excusable neglect, 可原谅的过失

Exempt, 豁免/免除

Exemption, 豁免/免除

Exhibit, 证据/提出证据/展出

Exhibit, defense's, 证据，辩方的

Existing order, 现有秩序

Exonerate, 确定无罪/免除责任

Expedite, 加速/有助于

Expeditor, 催料员

Expenses, 价钱/开支

Expert witness, 专家证人

Expire, 期满/失效/死亡

Expungement, 涂掉/省略

Extend, 延伸/提供

Extension, 延期/延长/扩大

Extenuating circumstances, 可使罪行减轻的情况

Extort, 敲诈/勒索

Extortion, 敲诈/勒索

Extracurricular, 课外的/业余的

Extradition, 引渡逃犯

Extrinsic, 外在的/非本质的

Eyewitness, 目击者

F

Facilitate, 促进/使便利

Fact, 事实

Factual basis, 事实依据

Factual contention, 事实性争论

Failure to, 未能/失败

Failure to appear, 未能出庭

Fair hearing, 公平聆讯

Fair market value, 公平市价

Fair settlement, 公平的解决方案

False imprisonment, 非法监禁

Family court, 家事法庭

Federal jurisdiction, 联邦司法管辖权

Fee, 费/酬金

Felon, 重罪犯

Felony, 重罪

Field sobriety Test, 现场清醒测试

File, 档案/提出/归档

File a complaint, 呈交诉状

File charges, 文件费

File number, 文件编号

File suit, 提起诉讼

Filed, 申请/存档

Filing, 文件归档/锉

Filing fee, 申请费

Financial screening, 经济审查

Finding, 调查/结果/（陪审团的）裁决

Fine, 好的/罚款

Finger print, 指纹

Fingerprinting, 指纹识别

Fire, 火/解雇

Firearm, 火器/枪炮

First degree, 一级

First name, 名

Flee, 逃走/飞逝

For the record, 供记录在案

Forcible rape, 强奸

Foreclosure, 抵押品赎回权的取消

Foregoing, 前面的/前述的

Forfeit bail, 保释后不如期出庭

Forfeiture of assets, 没收财产

Forgery, 伪造/伪造罪/赝品

Form, 形式/表格/产生

Foster, 领养/培养/促进

Foster care, 家庭寄养

Foster home, 寄养家庭

Foundation, 基础/基金会/创办

Fraud, 欺诈/诈骗

Freedom of speech, 言论自由

Freedom of the press, 出版自由

Fringe benefits, 附加福利

Frivolous, 轻薄的/轻率的

Full force, 全面生效/全力

Full time, 全职/全日制

Funding, 基金/给...拨款

Furlough, 休假/公休

G

Garnish, 装饰/传讯

Garnishment, 装饰/出庭传票/扣押债权的通知

General Assistance, 一般援助

Go to trial, 受审

Good faith, 善意

Government Center, 政府中心

Grand Jury, 大陪审团

Grant, 拨款/授予

Grant, 拨款/授予

Gross misdemeanor, 严重的轻罪

Gross wage, 工资总额

Ground/not grounds for, 有理由/无理由

Guardian, 监护人/保护人

Guardian ad litem, 法定监护人

Guardianship, 监护/保护

Guidelines, 指导方针/准则

Guilty plea, 有罪答辩

H

Habeas corpus, 人身保护令

Habitual offender, 惯犯

Halfway house,
康复之家（帮助人康复或清醒并重新融入社会的机构）

Handcuffs and leg-irons, 手铐和脚镣

Handicapped, 残疾的/有生理缺陷的

Harass, 骚扰

Harassment, 骚扰/烦恼

Harassment Order, 骚扰令

Hardened criminal, 惯犯/不知悔改的罪犯

Hazing, 受辱/被欺负

Head of Household, 户主

Health care, 卫生保健

Health insurance, 健康险

Hear a case, 审理案件

Hearing, 听到/审讯/听证会

Hearing officer, 听证官

Hearing, contested, 听证会，有争议的

Hearsay evidence, 非直接证据/传闻证据

Held without bail, 收押不得保释

Hereby, 因此/特此

Heroin, 海洛因

Hindering prosecution, 妨碍起诉

Hire, 租用/雇用

Hispanic, 西班牙的/西班牙语的/西班牙人的

Hit-and-run, 肇事后逃逸

Hold a hearing, 举行听证会

Holdup, 持枪抢劫/停顿

Holiday, 假期/节日

Home address, 家庭住址

Homicide, 杀人

Hostile witness, 恶意证人

House arrest, 软禁于家中

Household, 家庭

Household expense, 家庭开支

Household goods, 家庭用品

Housewife, 家庭主妇

Housing, 住房

Human resources, 人力资源

Hung jury, 未能作出裁定的陪审团

I

Illegal immigrant, 非法移民

Immigration, 移居/移民

Immigration and Customs Enforcement (ICE),
美国移民和海关执法局（ICE）

Immigration status, 移民身份/入境身份

Imminent, 临近的/逼近的

Immunity, 免疫/豁免

Impaired, 受损的

Impeach, 弹劾/控告

Impeachment, 弹劾/控告

Impeachment of witness, 弹劾证人

Implicate, 意味着/暗示

Implied consent advisory, 默示同意咨询

Impose, 强加于/处以

Impound, 扣押/没收/保管

Impound lot, 拖吊厂

Imprisoned, 被监禁/坐牢

Imprisonment, 监禁/关押

Improper motives, 不正当的动机

In fact, 事实上

In forma pauperis, 以贫民的身份免付诉讼费

Inadmissible, 不承认的/不允许的

Inadvertence, 不注意/疏忽

Inadvertent, 非故意的/疏忽的

Incidental, 偶然的/附带的

Income, 收入/收益

Income share guidelines, 收入分配指南

Income Tax, 所得税

Income tax refund, 所得税退税

Incriminate, 连累

Incur, 招致/引起

Indecent exposure, 有伤风化的暴露

Independent, 独立的/无关的

Indict, 控告/起诉

Indictment, 起诉/起诉状

Indigence, 贫穷

Indigent, 贫困的

Individualized, 个人的/有个人特色的

Ineligible, 无资格的/不适当的

Infant, 婴儿/初期的

Informal, 非正式的

Informant, 通知者/告密者

Information, 信息/通知

Infraction, 违法/违反

Inherit, 继承

Inheritance, 继承/遗产

Initial, 开始的/最初的

Initials, 首字母

Initiate legal proceedings, 提起法律诉讼

Injunction, 禁令/指令

Injure, 伤害/损害

Injury, 受伤处/损害

Inmate, 囚徒/被收容者

Innocent until proven guilty,

证据不足不能定罪/疑罪从无/无罪推定

Installment, 分期付款/安装

Insurance, 保险/保险费

Insured, 被保险的

Intact, 完好无缺的

Intake, 吸入/招收/入口

Interest (stake), 利息（股份）

Interest charging, 收取利息

Interest earned, 已取得的利息

Interest of justice, 维护正义

Interim, 临时的/中间的

Internal head injury, 头部内部受伤

Internal Revenue Service, 国税局

Intersection, 交集/十字路口

Intervenor, 干预者/介入者

Intoxilizer, 酒醉测试器

Intrinsic, 固有的/内在的

Invalidate, 使无效

Invest, 投资/授予

Investment, 投资/投资额

IRA (Individual Retirement Account), 个人退休账户

Irrelevant, 不相关的

Irretrievable breakdown of the marriage, 无可挽回的婚姻破裂

Issuance, 发行/发布

Issue, 问题/发行/颁布

Issue, 问题/发行/颁布

Item, 条/项目/物品

J

Jail, 监狱/看守所

Joint and several obligation, 连带责任

Joint child, 共同产物

Joint petition, 共同呈请书

Joyriding, 驾车兜风/偷车乱开罪

Judge, 法官/审批

Judgment, 判断/判决

Judgment for possession, 占有判决

Judicial, 司法的/公正的

Judicial District, 司法辖区

Judiciary, 司法的/法院的/法官的

Jump bail, 弃保潜逃

Jurisdiction, 司法权/管辖权

Juror, 陪审员

Jury, 陪审团

Jury box, 陪审席

Jury foreman/jury foreperson, 陪审团主席

Jury Room, 陪审团休息室

Jury trial, 由陪审团进行的审讯

Justice, 正义/司法

Juvenile, 青少年的/幼稚的

Juvenile court, 少年法庭

Juvenile delinquency, 青少年犯罪

Juvenile hall, 少管所

K

Kidnap, 绑架/诱拐

Kidnapping, 绑架/诱拐

Knowingly, 故意地

L

Landlord, 地主/房东

Larceny, 盗窃

Last known address, 最后为人所知的地址

Last name, 姓氏

Latent prints, 潜指纹

Later date, 晚些时候

Latin, 拉丁语/拉丁人

Law, 法律/定律

Law enforcement agencies, 执法机构

Law enforcement officer, 执法人员

Law Library, 法律图书馆

Law-abiding, 守法的

Lawful, 合法的

Lawsuit, 诉讼/控诉

Leading question, 有诱导性的提问

Lease, 租约/出租/租得

Legal Aid, 法律援助

Legal contentions, 法律辩论

Legal custodian, 法定监护人

Legal custody, 法定监护/保管

Legal separation, 合法分居

Legal Services, 法律服务

Legislature, 立法机关

Leniency, 宽大/仁慈

Lenient, 宽大的/仁慈的

Levy, 征税/税款

Liability, 责任/倾向/不利因素

License, 许可证/准许

Lie detector, 测谎器

Life imprisonment, 无期徒刑

Life in prison, 终生监禁

Life insurance policy, 寿险保单

Life sentence, 无期徒刑

Limited exception, 有限的例外

Limited liability, 有限责任

Limited liability corporation, 有限责任公司

Line-up, 使（排队）

Litigant, 诉讼当事人/诉讼的

Litigate, 诉讼

Litigation, 诉讼/起诉

Living expenses, 生活费

Living Will, 生前遗嘱

Loan, 贷款/借出

Location, 位置/场所

Loitering with intent, 蓄意作案

Long-term, 长期的

Long-term placement facility, 长期放置的设施

Loss, 损失/失败

Lot rent, 地段租金

Lure, 诱惑/吸引

Lynching, 处以私刑

M

Magistrate, 地方行政官/治安官

Maintenance order, 赡养判令

Malice, 预谋/恶意

Malicious Mischief, 故意损害他人财产

Malicious punishment of a child, 恶意惩罚儿童罪

Malpractice, 失职/行为不当

Malpractice insurance, 医疗事故保险

Manager, 经理/经纪人

Mandate, 命令/授权

Mandatory, 法定的/义务的

Mandatory minimum sentence, 刚性最低刑

Manslaughter, 过失杀人（罪）

Marijuana, 大麻

Marital, 婚姻的/夫妻的

Marital property, 婚姻财产

Marriage certificate, 结婚证

Married, 已婚的/婚姻的

Material evidence, 物证

Material witness, 能提供实质性证据的证人

Matter, 事情/物质/要紧

May it please the court,请允许我

Mediation, 调解/仲裁

Mediation services, 调解服务

Mediator, 调解人/中介人

Medical Assistance, 医疗援助

Medical history, 病史

Medical malpractice, 医疗事故

Medical record,病历

Medical support, 医疗支持

Mental abuse, 精神暴力

Mental health, 心理健康

Mental illness, 精神疾病

Mental retardation, 智力缺陷

Merit, 优点/价值/值得

Methamphetamine, 甲基苯丙胺

Middle name, 中间名

Minimum mandatory fine, 强制性最低罚款

Minimum payment, 最低支付额

Miranda rights, 米兰达权利

Misconduct, 行为不捡/管理或处理不当

Misdemeanor, 轻罪/不正当的行为

Misleading, 使误解/把...带错路

Mistrial, 无效审判/误判

Mitigating circumstances, 减轻罪行的情况

Mitigation hearing, 减刑听证会

Modify/modification, 修改/修改

Money laundering, 洗钱

Monitor, 监视/监督/班长

Monthly payment, 月付款额

Moral development, 道德发展

Motion, 运动/示意/动议

Motion to dismiss, 撤销案件动议

Municipal court, 市法院

Murder, 谋杀/损坏/谋杀案

Murder attempt,谋杀未遂

Murder weapon, 杀人凶器

Mutual benefit, 互惠互利

Mutually-agreed upon, 双方商定

N

Narcotics, 麻醉剂/麻醉毒品

Native American, 美洲印第安人

Necessary monthly expenses, 每月必要开支

Neglect, 忽略/忽视/疏忽

Negligence, 疏忽/渎职

Negotiate, 洽谈/协商

Net equity, 权益净额

No later than, 不迟于

No merit, 没有可取之处

No-contact order, 禁止接触令

Nolo contendere, 无罪申诉（刑事诉讼中，
被告不认罪但又放弃申辩）

Non compos mentis, 精神不正常的/心神丧失的

Non custodial parent, 非监护方家长

Non marital property,非婚姻财产

Noncompliance, 不服从/不顺从

Non-profit organization,非营利组织

Notarized, 经公证的

Notary public, 公证人

Notice, 注意/观察/通知

Notice of entry, 入监通知书

Notice of motions, 动议通知

Nuisance Oath, 滋扰誓言

Nurturance/Nurturing, 养成/培育

O

Oath, 誓言/誓约

Object, 物体/目的/反对

Objection, 反对/异议

Obligee, 债权人

Obligor, 债务人

Obnoxious, 可憎的/不愉快的

Obtain entry, 得到入境权

Off the record, 不供发表的/非正式的

Offender, 罪犯/冒犯者

Offense, 过错/犯罪/犯规

Offer of proof, 举证

Offset, 补偿/抵消

Omnibus hearing, 混合听审

On the record,记录在案的

Opening arguments, 开场辩论

Opening statement, 开场陈述

Oral copulation, forced, 口交，被迫的

Order, 命令/顺序

Order for protection, 保护令

Order to show cause, 陈述理由令

Original, 原始的/原版的/原创的

Out-of-court settlement, 庭外和解

Outstanding debts, 未偿清的债务

Overall, 全部的/总体来说

Overdose, （药物）过度剂量

Overrule, 驳回/否决

Oversight, 疏忽/监管

Overt act, 公开行为

Overtime, 超时的/加班的

Own, 自己的/特有的

Own recognizance, 自我担保

Owner, 物主/所有人

Ownership interest, 所有者权益

P

Paid, 已付款的

Pain and suffering, 疼痛和痛苦

Paraphernalia, 随身用品/已婚妇女的私人财产

Pardon, 赦免/原谅

Pardon extraordinary, 特赦

Parent, 家长/父母/根源

Parental rights, 亲权

Parenting time, 亲子时间

Parenting time expeditors, 亲子时间稽查员

Parole, 假释/（为获假释而作出的）誓言

Parole board, 假释委员会

Partially paid, 部分支付

Participate in, 参加/参与

Parties, 各方/当事人

Party, 一方/当事人/政党

Paternity, 父系/父子关系

Pay off, 偿清/贿赂

Pay stub, 工资单

Payable to, 支票抬头

Payables, 应付款项

Payment, 付款/报偿

PBT (preliminary breath test), 初步呼吸测试

Pedophile, 恋童癖

Penalty, 处罚/罚金

Penalty assessment, 附加罚金

Penalty of perjury, 伪证罪

Pending, 待定的/在…期间

Pending trial, 待审/候审

Pension, 养老金/抚恤金

Peremptory strike or challenge, 专横的罢工或挑战

Perjury, 伪证（罪）

Permanent resident, 永久性居民

Perpetrate, 犯罪/做坏事

Perpetrator, 犯人/作恶之人

Personal allowance, 计算所得税时的个人免税额

Personal injury, 人身伤害

Personal property, 个人财产

Personal recognizance, 个人担保

Personal security, 个人安全/人身担保

Personnel, 人员/员工/人事部门

Petit Jury, 小陪审团

Petition, 请愿书/诉状/申请

Petitioner, 请愿人/上诉人/离婚案原告

Petty misdemeanor, 轻罪/过失

Petty offense, 轻罪

Petty theft, 小偷小摸

Physical abuse, 身体虐待

Physical custody, 人身管束

Picture identification, 图像识别

Plaintiff, 原告

Plea, 抗辩/恳求/借口

Plea agreement, 认罪协议

Plea bargain, 辩诉交易

Plea negotiations, 认罪谈判

Plea of Guilty, 认罪

Plea of Innocence, 提出无罪抗辩

Plea of not-guilty, 无罪申诉

Plead, 申诉/答辩/辩护

Plead guilty/not guilty, 认罪/无罪申诉

Pleadings, 诉状/恳求

Police raid, 警方突袭

Police Station, 警察局

Polygraph, 测谎器

Post bail, 交保/提交保释金

Postpone, 推迟/延期

Postponement, 推迟

Pot, 大麻/锅

Power of attorney, 授权书

Practice, 练习/实践/惯例

Preceding, 在先的/在前的

Precluding, 阻止/排除

Predator, 食肉动物

Prejudice, 偏见/损害

Preliminary hearing, 预审程序

Preponderance of evidence, 证据优势

Prerogative writ, 紧急令/特权令

Preschooler, 学龄前儿童

Prescribed, 规定的/指定的

Present value, 现值

Pre-Sentence report, 量刑报告

Presumption of innocence, 无罪推定

Presumptive sentence, 标准推定刑

Pretrial, 审判前的

Pre-trial conference, 审前会议

Pre-trial motion, 审前动议

Pretrial offense, 审前犯罪

Prima facie, 表面的/明显的

Primary care giver, 主要照料者

Principal assets, 主要财产

Print, 印刷/出版

Printout, 打印输出

Priors, 优先的/在前的

Prison, 监狱

Prisoner, 囚徒

Privacy, 隐私

Private health care coverage, 私人医疗保险

Privilege, 特权/优惠

Probable cause, 可能的原因

Probate, 遗嘱查验/遗嘱查讫证

Probation, 缓刑/试用期

Probation officer, 缓刑监督官

Procedural, 程序的

Procedure, 程序/步骤

Proceeding, 程序/诉讼

Proceedings, 程序/诉讼

Process, 过程/程序

Pronounce sentence, 宣判

Proof, 证据/证明

Proper notice, 适当的注意/适当的通知

Property, 财产/物业

Proportionate share, 按比例应占的份额

Prosecute, 起诉/告发

Prosecute, 起诉/告发

Prosecution, 起诉/原告

Prosecutor, 公诉人/检举人

Protection Order, 保护令

Prove, 证明/结果是

Proving, 证明/结果是

Provisional license, 临时执照

Public assistance, 政府援助

Public defender, 公设辩护人

Public notice/warning, 通告

Public nuisance, 公共滋扰

Public's interest, 公众的利益

Punishable, 该罚的/可罚的

Pursuant, 根据

Pursuant to, 根据/依照

Q

Qualified, 有资格的

Quarter, 四分之一/一个季度/一刻钟

Quash, 平息/镇压

Quit claim deed, 放弃索偿契约

R

Range of costs, 成本范围

Rape, 强奸

Rape, statutory, 强奸，法定的

Rationale, 基本原理/根据

Real estate, 不动产

Reasonable doubt, 合理的怀疑

Rebuttal, 反驳/反证

Recess, 暂停/休庭

Reckless, 不计后果的/大意的

Reckless driving, 鲁莽驾驶

Reckless endangerment, 怠忽危害罪

Record, 记录

Recusal, 宣布不合格/取消资格

Recuse, 取消资格/要求撤换

Redirect examination, 再次直接询问

Reduce, 减少/缩小

Reduction, 减少/缩小

Refer, 参考/引用

Referee, 裁判员/仲裁人

Refund, 退款

Rehabilitate, 改造/修复

Reimburse, 偿还/报销

Relationship, 关系/关联

Relative, 亲属/相对的

Relative(s), 亲属

Relevant, 有关的/切题的

Relief, 轻松/缓解

Remain silent, 保持沉默

Remedy, 救济/治疗法/药物

Remit/remittance, 汇款

Render a verdict, 交付宣判

Rental agreement, 租赁协议

Repeat offender, 累犯

Repeat violation, 再犯

Replevin, 财物的发还

Report, 报告/告发

Repossession, 收回/重新占有

Request, 请求/要求

Request, 请求/要求

Required, 必需的

Reserve, 保留/预定

Residence, 住处/居住

Resisting arrest, 拒捕

Respond or object, 响应或反对

Respondent, 被告

Rest the case, 停止对该案提出证据

Restitution, 赔偿

Restraining order, 禁令

Restraints, 限制/抑制

Retirement benefits, 退休金

Retroactive, 有追溯力的

Return a verdict, 作出裁决

Revenue recapture, 收入收回

Review, 审查/审核/复习

Review hearing, 复核聆讯

Revocation, 废除/取消

Revoke, 撤销/取消

Right, 权利/右

Right of allocution, 训示权

Right to bear arms, 携带武器的权利

Riot, 暴乱/聚众闹事

Rioter, 暴民/喝酒狂闹的人

Risk factor, 风险因素

Robbery, 抢劫

Roommate, 室友

Routing Number, 路由号码

Rule, 规则/条例/统治

Rules, 规则/规章

Rules of Evidence, 证据规则

Rules/Regulations, 规章/条例

Ruling, 裁决/统治的

S

Sanction, 批准/处罚/制裁

Sanction, 批准/处罚/制裁

Scene, 情景/地点/景色

Schedule, 日程/安排

Scheduled, 预先安排的

School, 学校/学业

Screening, 筛选/选拔/遮蔽

Seal, 封条/印章/盖印

Seal the records, 密封记录

Search, 搜查/调查

Search, 搜查/调查

Search and Seizure, 搜查与扣押

Search warrant, 搜查令

Seasonal employment, 季节性就业

Second degree, 第二学位/硕士学位

Seize, 抓住/没收

Seizure, 没收/抵押

Seizure of assets, 扣押财产

Self-defense, 自卫/正当防卫

Self-employment, 自雇

Self-incrimination, 自证其罪

Self-worth, 自尊

Sentence, 宣判/句子

Sentence, 宣判/句子

Sentence to service, 服务刑

Sentence, concurrent, 合并服刑

Sentence, suspended, 缓刑

Sentences, consecutive, 连续判决

Sentencing guidelines, 量刑指南

Sentencing hearing, 量刑听证会

Separated, 分开的/个别的

Separation, 分离/分居

Separation anxiety, 分离焦虑

Sequester the Jury, 封存陪审团

Serial killer, 连环杀手

Serve, 服役/接待

Service, 服务/服役

Service of process, 传票送达

Session, 会议/会期

Set forth, 陈述/阐明

Set over, 移交

Settle, 解决/和解/定居

Settlement, 解决/结算/安置

Settlement conference, 和解会议

Sever, 切断/脱离

Sexual abuse, 性虐待

Sexual assault, 性侵犯

Sexual Assault, 性侵犯

Sexual offender, 性罪犯

Sexual offender treatment, 性罪犯治疗

Sexual offense, 性犯罪

Sexual predator, 性侵犯者

Sheriff, 郡治安官

Shoot, 射击/开枪/拍照

Shoot to death, 枪杀

Shoplifting, 入店行窃

Short-term, 短期的

Shotgun, 猎枪/强迫的/漫无目的的

Show Cause hearing, 陈述理由听证会

Show Cause order, 陈述理由令

Sidebar, 补充报道/法官与即将受审案件的律师间的会晤

Sign, 签署/标记/手势

Significant, 重要的/有意义的

Significant issue, 重大问题

Single, 单一的/单个的

Small Claims, 小额索偿

Small claims court, 小额索偿法院

Sober, 清醒的/稳重的

Social Security Number, 社会保险号

Speed limit, 速度限制

Speeding, 超速行驶/高速行驶

Speedy trial, 快速审理

Spousal maintenance, （离婚后丈夫给妻子的）赡养费

Spouse, 配偶

SSI, 补充保障收入

Stab, 刺/尝试

Staggered Sentencing, 交错量刑

Stalking, 跟踪/茎

Stand down, 退出（比赛或竞选）/（从某职位上）退下

Standard sentencing range, 量刑标准范围

Statute, 成文法/规则

Statute of limitations, 时效

Statutory rape, 法定强奸罪

Stay, 保持/延缓

Stay of adjudication, 待裁决的

Step-Family, 有继父（或继母）的家庭

Step-son, mother, father, etc., 继子，继母, 继父等

Stipulate, 规定

Stipulation, 规定/约定

Stock(s), 股票

Strike, 罢工/打击

Student loan, 助学贷款

Submit, 听从/提交

Submitted, 听从

Subpoena, 传票

Subscribed and sworn, 签字并宣誓

Successfully complete, 成功完成

Sue, 控告/起诉/请求

Sufficient, 足够的/充分的

Suit, 诉讼/请求/适合/满足

Suitable age, 适格年龄

Summary dissolution, 简易离婚

Summary judgment, 简易判决

Summation, 总结/总和

Summon, 召唤/召集/传票

Summoned, 受到召唤的

Summons, 传票/传唤

Summons and Complaint, 传票和诉状

Supervised release, 监外看管

Support, 支持/拥护

Supporting documents, 支持性文件

Suppress evidence, 隐匿证据

Supreme Court, 最高法院

Surcharge, 额外费用/过高的要价

Suspect, 推测/怀疑/可疑的/嫌疑犯

Suspected of Swear, **涉嫌**发誓

Suspended, 被暂时搁置的

Suspended sentence, 缓刑

Sustained, 持久的/经久不衰的

Sworn, 发过誓的

T

Take an oath, 宣誓

Take judicial notice of, 采取司法认知的

Take-home pay, 扣税后的实得工资

Tax, 税/征税

Tax offset, 税收抵消

Teenager, 青少年/13岁到19岁的年轻人

Temporary, 暂时的/临时的

Temporary restraining order, 临时限制令

Tenant, 承租人/占用者/租赁

Tenure, 终身职位/任期

Terminal illness, 晚期病症

Terminate, 停止/终止

Terms and conditions, 条款和条件

Terroristic threats, 恐怖性威胁

Testify, 作证/证明

Testimony, 证词/见证

Theft, 偷窃/失窃

Third party, 第三方

Threat, 威胁/恐吓

Threaten, 威胁/预示

Ticket, 车票/罚款/传票

Time share, 限时产权

Title, 题目/称号/权益

To the best of your knowledge and belief, 据你所知和所信的

To the letter of the law, 根据法律的字面意思

Toddler, 初学走路的孩子

Traffic, 交通/（非法）交易

Transcript, 抄本/成绩单/笔录

Trespass, 侵犯/闯入私人领地

Trespasser, 侵入者/侵犯者

Trespassing, 非法入侵

Trial, 审讯/试验

Tribunal, 法庭/法官席/法院

Truancy, 逃学/玩忽职守

Truant, 旷课者

True and correct, 真实和正确的

Tutorial, 指南/教程/辅导的

U

Unconditional release, 无条件释放

Under oath, 宣过誓

Under penalty of, 违者受...的处罚

Under way, 在进行中

Undercover agent, 警方密探

Underlying Crime or offense, 潜在犯罪

Undersigned, 署名者/在下面签字的

Undue, 过分的/不适当的

Unemployment, 失业/失业人数

Unemployment compensation, 失业补偿金

Uninsured, 未投保险的

Universal life insurance, 综合人寿保险

Unlawful harassment, 非法骚扰

Unpaid, 未付的/未缴纳的

Unreasonable, 不合理的/不切实际的

Unreimbursed, 未偿还的

Unsupervised Probation, 非监督缓刑

US Department of Labor, 美国劳工部

Usually, 通常/平常

Utilities, 功用/效用

V

Vacate, 空出/让出

Value, 价值/重要性

Vandalism, 故意破坏公物的行为

Vehicular assault, 驾车攻击罪

Vehicular homicide, 车祸致人死亡罪

Vehicular manslaughter, 交通肇事杀人罪

Venue, 审判地/会场/犯罪地点

Verbatim, 逐字的

Verdict, 裁定/裁决/定论

Verify, 核实/证实

Versus, 对抗/与...相对

Veteran, 老兵/经验丰富的人

Veteran's benefits, 退伍年金

Violate, 违反/侵犯/妨碍

Violation, 违反/妨碍

Violations bureau, 违规局

Visitation rights, 探视权

Voluntarily, 自愿地/自动地

W

Waive, 放弃/推迟/搁置

Waive rights, 放弃权利

Waiver, 放弃/弃权证书

Wanton, 无节制的/肆无忌惮的

Warning, 警告/警报/预兆

Warrant, 授权令/证明是正当的

Warrant, arrest, 授权令，逮捕

Warrant, bench, 拘票，法院

Warrant, search, 授权令，搜查

Warranted, 担保的/保证的

Warranty, 担保书/保修期/保单

Weapon, 武器/兵器

Weapon, concealed, 武器，隐藏的

Weapon, deadly, 武器，致命的

Weight of evidence, 证明力

Welfare, 福利/福利事业/幸福

Well grounded, 正当的/有根据的

Whereabouts, 下落/所在之处

Whereas, 然而/但是

Whole life insurance, 终身寿险

Will, 遗嘱

Willful, 任性的/故意的

Willful act, 蓄意行为

Willfully, 蓄意地/任性故意地

Willing, 乐意的/心甘情愿的

With prejudice, 有偏见/有损

With regard to, 关于/就...而论

Without prejudice, 无偏见/不受损害

Witness, 证人/证言/目击

Witness stand, 证人席

Witness, defense, 证人, 辩方

Witness, expert, 证人, 专家

Witness, hostile, 证人, 恶意

Witness, material, 证人, 能提供实质性证据的

Witness, prosecution, 证人, 控方

Work furlough, 暂准监外工作

Work release, 白天监外工作

Work/Study release, 白天监外工作/学习

Worker's compensation, 工伤赔偿金

Writ, 令状/书面命令

Writ of execution, 执行令状

Wrongful death, 过失致人死亡

Wrongful denial, **不当拒**绝

CHINESE-ENGLISH
中文—英语

安排/整理, Arrangement

按比例应占的份额, Proportionate share

按照, According to

案件编号, Case number

案件陈述, Brief

案件类型, Case type

罢工/打击, Strike

白天监外工作, Work release

白天监外工作/学习, Work/Study release

绑架/诱拐, Kidnap

绑架/诱拐, Kidnapping

保持/延缓, Stay

保持沉默, Remain silent

保护令, Order for protection

保护令, Protection Order

保留/预定, Reserve

保姆, Baby sitting

保释/保释金/担保人, Bail

保释担保人, Bail bondsman

保释后不如期出庭, Forfeit bail

保释金, Bail bond

保释金没收, Bail forfeiture

保释审查, Bail review

保险/保险费, Insurance

保证金要求, Bond requirement

保证人, Bondsman

报告/告发, Report

暴乱/聚众闹事, Riot

暴民/喝酒狂闹的人, Rioter

被保险的, Insured

被告, Defendant

被告, Respondent

被告/被指控的, Accused

被监禁/坐牢, Imprisoned

被拘留的/扣押的, Detained

被收养的/被采纳的, Adopt(ed)

被暂时搁置的, Suspended

苯丙胺, Amphetamine

必需的, Required

辩护/防卫, Defense

辩护律师, Defense attorney

辩论/理由/论证, Argument

辩诉交易, Plea bargain

标准/准则, Criteria

标准推定刑, Presumptive sentence

表面的/明显的, Prima facie

病历, Medical record

病史, Medical history

摒弃/没有...也行, Dispense with

拨款/授予, Grant

拨款/授予, Grant

剥夺, Depriving

驳回/否决, Overrule

驳回的/摒弃的, Dismissed

驳回索赔, Dismiss a claim

驳回指控, Dismiss a charge

补偿/抵消, Offset

补偿性亲子时间, Compensatory parenting time

补充保障收入, SSI

补充报道/法官与即将受审案件的律师间的会晤, Sidebar

不成比例的高成本, Disproportionately high costs

不承认的/不允许的, Inadmissible

不迟于, No later than

不当拒绝, Wrongful denial

不动产, Real estate

不服从/不顺从, Noncompliance

不供发表的/非正式的, Off the record

不合理的/不切实际的, Unreasonable

不计后果的/大意的, Reckless

不相关的, Irrelevant

不一致/争论, Disagreement

不在场证据/托辞, Alibi

不正当的动机, Improper motives

不注意/疏忽, Inadvertence

部分支付, Partially paid

财产/房地产, Estate

财产/物业, Property

财物的发还, Replevin

裁定/裁决/定论, Verdict

裁决/统治的, Ruling

裁量权/谨慎, Discretion

裁判员/仲裁人, Referee

采取司法认知的, Take judicial notice of

参加/参与, Participate in

参考/引用, Refer

残疾的/有生理缺陷的, Handicapped

残障的, Disabled

测谎器, Lie detector

测谎器, Polygraph

尝试/努力, Attempt

偿还/报销, Reimburse

偿清/贿赂, Pay off

抄本/成绩单/笔录, Transcript

超出合理怀疑, Beyond a reasonable doubt

超时的/加班的, Overtime

超速行驶/高速行驶, Speeding

车祸致人死亡罪, Vehicular homicide

车票/罚款/传票, Ticket

撤销/取消, Revoke

撤销案件动议, Motion to dismiss

沉溺/上瘾的, Addict

陈述/阐明, Set forth

陈述理由令, Order to show cause

陈述理由令, Show Cause order

陈述理由听证会, Show Cause hearing

成本/花费, Costs

成本范围, Range of costs

成功完成, Successfully complete

成人拘留中心, Adult Detention Center

成文法/规则, Statute

呈交诉状, File a complaint

承认/告知收到/表示感谢, Acknowledge

承认/允许, Admit

承租人/占用者/租赁, Tenant

程序/步骤, Procedure

程序/诉讼, Proceeding

程序/诉讼, Proceedings

程序的, Procedural

迟延起诉, Deferred prosecution

迟滞/欠款, Arrearage

持久的/经久不衰的, Sustained

持枪抢劫/停顿, Holdup

持械抢劫, Armed robbery

出版自由, Freedom of the press

出生日期, Date of birth

出生证明, Birth certificate

出现, Appear

出现/外观, Appearance

初步呼吸测试, PBT (preliminary breath test)

初学走路的孩子, Toddler

处罚/罚金, Penalty

处理/交易, Deal

处以私刑, Lynching

传票, Subpoena

传票/传唤, Summons

传票和诉状, Summons and Complaint

传票送达, Service of process

吹/殴打, Blow

此时, At this time

刺/尝试, Stab

促进/使便利, Facilitate

催料员, Expeditor

DNA样本, DNA sample

答辩/答辩状, Answer

打印输出, Printout

大麻, Marijuana

大麻/锅, Pot

大陪审团, Grand Jury

逮捕/拘留/吸引, Arrest

逮捕记录, Arrest record

逮捕令/拘票, Arrest warrant

贷款/借出, Loan

待裁决的, Stay of adjudication

待定的/在...期间, Pending

待审/候审, Pending trial

怠忽危害罪, Reckless endangerment

担保的/保证的, Warranted

担保书/保修期/保单, Warranty

单据/备审案件目录, Docket

单一的/单个的, Single

弹道学报告, Ballistics report

弹劾/控告, Impeach

弹劾/控告, Impeachment

弹劾证人, Impeachment of witness

当前的/流行的, Current(ly)

当事人(辩护人)对己方证人作的初步询问, Direct examination

档案/提出/归档, File

盗车, Car theft

盗车罪, Auto theft

盗窃, Burglary

盗窃, Larceny

盗用/侵吞, Embezzlement

道德发展, Moral development

道德沦丧罪, Crimes of moral turpitude

得到入境权, Obtain entry

抵押品赎回权的取消, Foreclosure

地段租金, Lot rent

地方行政官/治安官, Magistrate

地址/处理/讲话, Address

地址/处理/讲话, Address

地址/处理/讲话, Address

地主/房东, Landlord

递延收益, Deferred Income

第二学位/硕士学位, Second degree

第三方, Third party

电子家庭监控, Electronic home monitoring

动议通知, Notice of motions

独立的/无关的, Independent

短期的, Short-term

断言/主张/指控, Allegation

断言/主张/指控, Allege

对抗/与...相对, Versus

对抗性证人, Adversarial witness

额外费用/过高的要价, Surcharge

恶意惩罚儿童罪, Malicious punishment of a child

恶意证人, Hostile witness

儿童, Child

儿童, Children

儿童保育, Child Care

儿童保育协助, Child Care assistance

儿童的最大利益, Child's Best Interest

发过誓的, Sworn

发行/发布, Issuance

发现/发觉/发现物, Discovery

发展的, Developmental

法案；行动, Act

法定的/义务的, Mandatory

法定监护/保管, Legal custody

法定监护人, Guardian ad litem

法定监护人, Legal custodian

法定强奸罪, Statutory rape

法定诉讼程序, Due process

法官, Bench

法官/审批, Judge

法官审理/法庭审理, Bench trial/Court trial

法官审理/无陪审员的审判, Bench trial

法警/区镇的地方长官, Bailiff

法律/定律, Law

法律辩论, Legal contentions

法律服务, Legal Services

法律顾问表, Counsel table

法律图书馆, Law Library

法律援助, Legal Aid

法庭, Court house

法庭, court room

法庭/法官席/法院, Tribunal

法庭/法院/院子, Court

法庭保卫, Court officer

法庭记录, Court Record

法院，区, Court, District

法院，少年, Court, Juvenile

法院档案编号, Court File Number

法院翻译员, Court interpreter

法院副管理员, Deputy Court Administrator

法院管理员, Court Administrator

法院拘票, Bench warrant

法院书记官, Court reporter

法院指定的律师, Court appointed attorney

法院指令, Court order

反驳/反证, Rebuttal

反对/异议, Objection

反诉, Counterclaim

反向动议, Counter motion

犯人/作恶之人, Perpetrator

犯罪/委托/承诺, Commit

犯罪/委托/承诺, Commit

犯罪/罪行, Crime

犯罪/罪行, Crime

犯罪/做坏事, Perpetrate

犯罪记录/历史, Criminal record/history

犯罪浪潮, Crime wave

犯罪时正患精神病者, Criminal insanity

犯罪史, Criminal history

犯罪事实, Corpus delicti

犯罪现场, Crime scene

犯罪性行为, Criminal sexual conduct

犯罪性接触, Criminal sexual contact

防弹, Bulletproof

防弹背心, Bulletproof vest

妨碍起诉, Hindering prosecution

放弃/弃权证书, Waiver

放弃/推迟/搁置, Waive

放弃权利, Waive rights

放弃索偿契约, Quit claim deed

放弃指控, Drop the charge

非法监禁, False imprisonment

非法入侵, Trespassing

非法骚扰, Unlawful harassment

非法移民, Illegal immigrant

非故意的/疏忽的, Inadvertent

非婚姻财产, Non marital property

非监督缓刑, Unsupervised Probation

非监护方家长, Non custodial parent

非营利组织, Non-profit organization

非正式的, Informal

非直接证据/传闻证据, Hearsay evidence

废除/取消, Revocation

废除/宣告无效, Annul

费/酬金, Fee

分开的/个别的, Separated

分离/分居, Separation

分离/离婚, Divorce

分离焦虑, Separation anxiety

分流方案, Diversion Program

分配/分派, Allocate(d)

分期付款/安装, Installment

风险因素, Risk factor

封存陪审团, Sequester the Jury

封条/印章/盖印, Seal

否决动议, Deny a motion

否决亲子时间, Deny parenting time

否认/拒绝, Denial

否认/拒绝, Deny

夫妻间的殴打威胁, Battery, spousal

服从/遵守, Compliance

服务/服役, Service

服务刑, Sentence to service

服役/接待, Serve

福利/福利事业/幸福, Welfare

父系/父子关系, Paternity

付款/报偿, Payment

附加的/依恋的, Attached

附加罚金, Penalty assessment

附加福利, Fringe benefits

复核聆讯, Review hearing

副职/代表, Deputy

该罚的/可罚的, Punishable

改造/修复, Rehabilitate

干预者/介入者, Intervenor

刚性最低刑, Mandatory minimum sentence

告诫/提醒, Admonish

个人安全/人身担保, Personal security

个人财产, Personal property

个人担保, Personal recognizance

个人的/有个人特色的, Individualized

个人退休账户, IRA (Individual Retirement Account)

各方/当事人, Parties

根据, Pursuant

根据/依照, Pursuant to

根据法律的字面意思, To the letter of the law

跟踪/茎, Stalking

工伤赔偿金, Worker's compensation

工资单, Pay stub

工资总额, Gross wage

公共安全部, Deptartment of Public Safety

公共滋扰, Public nuisance

公开行为, Overt act

公平的/平等的, Equitable/Equal

公平的解决方案, Fair settlement

公平聆讯, Fair hearing

公平市价, Fair market value

公设辩护人, Public defender

公诉人/检举人, Prosecutor

公证人, Notary public

公众的利益, Public's interest

功用/效用, Utilities

攻击/抨击, Assault

共犯, Accomplice

共同产物, Joint child

共同呈请书, Joint petition

供记录在案, For the record

构成/制定, Constitute

估计/估价, Estimate

估计/评估, Assessment

股票, Stock(s)

固有的/内在的, Intrinsic

故意地, Knowingly

故意破坏公物的行为, Vandalism

故意损害他人财产, Malicious Mischief

顾问/律师, Counselor

雇主, Employer

雇主识别号码, Employer Identification Number

怪异的行为, Bizarre behavior

关系/关联, Relationship

关于/就...而论, With regard to

惯犯, Habitual offender

惯犯/不知悔改的罪犯, Hardened criminal

规定, Stipulate

规定/约定, Stipulation

规定的/指定的, Prescribed

规则/规章, Rules

规则/条例/统治, Rule

规章/条例, Rules/Regulations

国税局, Internal Revenue Service

过程/程序, Process

过错/犯罪/犯规, Offense

过度剂量（药物）, Overdose

过分的/不适当的, Undue

过分的/惊人的, Egregious

过失杀人（罪）, Manslaughter

过失致人死亡, Wrongful death

海洛因, Heroin

好辩的/有争议的, Contentious

好的/罚款, Fine

合并服刑, Sentence, concurrent

合并判刑, Concurrent sentences

合成制图, Composite drawing

合法的, Lawful

合法分居, Legal separation

合格/有资格, Eligibility

合理的怀疑, Reasonable doubt

和解会议, Settlement conference

核对/扣款, Check off

核实/证实, Verify

呼吸测醉器, Breathalyzer

忽略/忽视/疏忽, Neglect

互惠互利, Mutual benefit

户主, Head of Household

划界/界限, Bound

化学药品依赖, Chemical dependency

缓和/消除, Abate

缓刑, Sentence, suspended

缓刑, Suspended sentence

缓刑/试用期, Probation

缓刑监督官, Probation officer

毁坏/损害赔偿（金）, Damages

汇款, Remit/remittance

会计, Accounting

会计账簿, Accounting books

会议/会期, Session

贿赂, Bribe

贿赂, Bribery

婚姻财产, Marital property

婚姻的/夫妻的, Marital

混合听审, Omnibus hearing

豁免/免除, Exempt

豁免/免除, Exemption

火/解雇, Fire

火器/枪炮, Firearm

基本原理/根据, Rationale

基础/基金会/创办, Foundation

基础/原则, Basis

基金/给...拨款, Funding

基于, Based on

疾病治疗后的调养, Aftercare

计算/视为, Count

计算所得税时的个人免税额, Personal allowance

记录, Record

记录在案的, On the record

季节性就业, Seasonal employment

继承, Inherit

继承/遗产, Inheritance

继续, Continuance

继续, Continue

继子，继母, 继父等, Step-son, mother, father, etc.

寄养家庭, Foster home

加速/有助于, Expedite

加重的, Aggravated

加重罪行的情况, Circumstances, aggravating

家事法庭, Family court

家庭, Household

家庭暴力, Domestic abuse

家庭暴力, Domestic violence

家庭暴力级别, Domestic abuse classes

家庭寄养, Foster care

家庭开支, Household expense

家庭用品, Household goods

家庭主妇, Housewife

家庭住址, Home address

家长/父母/根源, Parent

甲基苯丙胺, Methamphetamine

假定/担任, Assume

假定/担任, Assumption

假期/节日, Holiday

假释, Conditional release

假释/（为获假释而作出的）誓言, Parole

假释委员会, Parole board

价钱/开支, Expenses

价值/重要性, Value

驾车兜风/偷车乱开罪, Joyriding

驾车攻击罪, Vehicular assault

驾驶记录, Driving record

驾驶执照, Driving permit

监管链, Chain of custody

监护/保护, Guardianship

监护/拘留, Custody

监护人/保护人, Guardian

监禁/关押, Imprisonment

监禁的/保管的, Custodial

监视/监督/班长, Monitor

监外看管, Supervised release

监狱, Prison

监狱/看守所, Jail

检查（制度）, Censorship

减轻罪行的情况, Circumstances, mitigating

减轻罪行的情况, Mitigating circumstances

减少/缩小, Reduce

减少/缩小, Reduction

减刑听证会, Mitigation hearing

简易离婚, Summary dissolution

简易判决, Summary judgment

建立/机构, Establishment

建议的权利, Advice of rights

建议性的/劝告的, Advisory

健康险, Health insurance

交保/提交保释金, Post bail

交错量刑, Staggered Sentencing

交付宣判, Render a verdict

交换/代偿/减刑, Commutation

交集/十字路口, Intersection

交通/（非法）交易, Traffic

交通肇事杀人罪, Vehicular manslaughter

教唆/怂恿, Abet

教唆/协谋, Aid and abet

接纳为证据, Admit into evidence

揭露/公开, Disclose

劫车, Carjacking

结案陈词, Closing argument

结果/引起, Effect

结合/债券, Bond

结婚证, Marriage certificate

解除, Dissolution

解除租赁, Break the lease

解雇/驳回, Dismiss

解决/和解/定居, Settle

解决/结算/安置, Settlement

紧急令/特权令, Prerogative writ

进入/登记, Enter

禁令, Restraining order

禁令/指令, Injunction

禁止接触令, No-contact order

经公证的, Notarized

经济审查, Financial screening

经理/经纪人, Manager

经认证的, Certified

精神暴力, Mental abuse

精神不正常的/心神丧失的, Non compos mentis

精神疾病, Mental illness

警察局, Police Station

警方密探, Undercover agent

警方突袭, Police raid

警告/警报/预兆, Warning

酒后驾车（极度兴奋时驾车/能力受损时驾车/酒后驾车），
DWI/DUI (Driving while intoxicated while impaired/Driving under
the influence)

酒后驾车, Drunk driving

酒后驾车, DUI

酒精传感器, Alcohol sensor

酒精呼气测试, Breath alcohol test

酒醉测试器, Intoxilizer

救济/治疗法/药物, Remedy

拘票，法院, Warrant, bench

举行听证会, Hold a hearing

举证, Offer of proof

举证责任, Burden of proof

拒捕, Resisting arrest

据你所知和所信的, To the best of your knowledge and belief

郡检察官, County Attorney

郡检察官办公室, County Attorney's Office

郡看守所, County jail

郡治安官, Sheriff

开场辩论, Opening arguments

开场陈述, Opening statement

开始的/最初的, Initial

看护者, Caregiver

康复之家（帮助人康复或清醒并重新融入社会的机构），Halfway house

抗辩/恳求/借口, Plea

考虑/关心/对价, Consideration

可加强的罪行, Enhanceable offense

可加重罪行的情况, Aggravating circumstances

可加重罪行的情况, Aggravating circumstances

可接纳的, Admissible

可接纳的证据, Admissible evidence

可卡因, Cocaine

可能的原因, Probable cause

可使罪行减轻的情况, Extenuating circumstances

可原谅的过失, Excusable neglect

可憎的/不愉快的, Obnoxious

课外的/业余的, Extracurricular

空出/让出, Vacate

恐怖性威胁, Terroristic threats

控告/起诉, Indict

控告/起诉/请求, Sue

控告起诉书, Accusatory instrument

口交，被迫的, Oral copulation, forced

扣除/推理, Deduction

扣税后的实得工资, Take-home pay

扣押/没收/保管, Impound

扣押财产, Seizure of assets

快速审理, Speedy trial

宽大/仁慈, Leniency

宽大的/仁慈的, Lenient

旷课者, Truant

拉丁语/拉丁人, Latin

蓝皮书, Blue Book

蓝皮书值, Blue Book Value

滥用/诽谤, Abuse

滥用者, Abuser

老兵/经验丰富的人, Veteran

乐意的/心甘情愿的, Willing

累犯, Repeat offender

累积/累计, Accrue/accruing

立法机关, Legislature

利息（股份）, Interest (stake)

利益/保险金, Benefits

利益冲突, Conflict of interest

连带责任, Joint and several obligation

连环杀手, Serial killer

连接体, Body attachment

连累, Incriminate

连续判决, Consecutive sentences

联邦司法管辖权, Federal jurisdiction

练习/实践/惯例, Practice

恋童癖, Pedophile

量刑报告, Pre-Sentence report

量刑标准范围, Standard sentencing range

量刑听证会, Sentencing hearing

量刑指南, Sentencing guidelines

列管药物, Controlled substance

猎枪/强迫的/漫无目的的, Shotgun

临近的/逼近的, Imminent

临时的/中间的, Interim

临时限制令, Temporary restraining order

临时执照, Provisional license

领养/培养/促进, Foster

令状/书面命令, Writ

流产/堕胎, Abortion

鲁莽驾驶, Reckless driving

路由号码, Routing Number

律师, Attorney

律师/法律顾问/劝告, Counsel

律师协会, Bar association

麻醉剂/麻醉毒品, Narcotics

没收/充公, Confiscate

没收/抵押, Seizure

没收财产, Forfeiture of assets

没有可取之处, No merit

每月必要开支, Necessary monthly expenses

美国劳工部, US Department of Labor

美国劳工统计局, Bureau of Labor Statistics

美国移民和海关执法局（ICE）, Immigration and Customs Enforcement (ICE)

美洲印第安人, Native American

猛击/打坏, Batter

米兰达权利, Miranda rights

秘密的/担任机密工作的, Confidential

密封记录, Seal the records

密谋/共谋, Conspiracy

免疫/豁免, Immunity

免职/驳回/拒绝受理, Dismissal

蔑视动议, Contempt motion

民事处罚, Civil penalties

民事公证, Civil Law Notary

民事拘禁令, Civil commitment

民事权利, Civil rights

民事诉讼, Civil action

名, First name

明确和令人信服的证据, Clear and convincing evidence

明显的, Conspicuous

命令/禁止, Enjoin

命令/授权, Mandate

命令/顺序, Order

默示同意咨询, Implied consent advisory

谋杀/损坏/谋杀案, Murder

谋杀未遂, Murder attempt

目击者, Eyewitness

那个时候, At that time

脑死亡, Brain death

能力评估, Competency evaluation

能提供实质性证据的证人, Material witness

年金/养老金, Annuity

年龄/时代, Age

虐待儿童, Child abuse

殴打, Battery

殴打/人身攻击, Assault and battery

偶然的/附带的, Incidental

盘问/交叉询问, Cross examination

盘问/交叉询问, Cross-examine

判断/判决, Judgment

判决/命令, Decree

判决/宣判, Adjudicate

判决/宣判, Adjudicating

判决/宣判, Adjudication

旁证/间接证据, Circumstantial evidence

陪审团, Jury

陪审团休息室, Jury Room

陪审团主席, Jury foreman/jury foreperson

陪审席, Jury box

陪审员, Juror

赔偿, Restitution

配件/同谋, Accessory

配偶, Spouse

批准/处罚/制裁, Sanction

偏见/损害, Prejudice

偏见宣誓书, Affidavit of prejudice

贫困的, Indigent

贫穷, Indigence

平等的保护, Equal protection

平行的/附属的, Collateral

平衡/天平/制衡, Balance

平息/镇压, Quash

破产/倒闭, Bankruptcy

破门而入, Breaking and entering

期满/失效/死亡, Expire

欺诈/诈骗, Fraud

起诉/告发, Prosecute

起诉/告发, Prosecute

起诉/起诉状, Indictment

起诉/原告, Prosecution

弃保潜逃, Jump bail

弃保潜逃/保释中逃走, Bail jumping

汽车险, Car insurance

洽谈/协商, Negotiate

签署/标记/手势, Sign

签字并宣誓, Subscribed and sworn

前面的/前述的, Foregoing

前述的, Aforementioned

潜逃/逃匿, Abscond

潜逃者, Absconder

潜在犯罪, Underlying Crime or offense

潜指纹, Latent prints

枪杀, Shoot to death

强加于/处以, Impose

强奸, Forcible rape

强奸, Rape

强奸，法定的, Rape, statutory

强制性最低罚款, Minimum mandatory fine

抢劫, Robbery

抢劫银行, Bank robbery

敲诈/勒索, Extort

敲诈/勒索, Extortion

切断/脱离, Sever

侵犯/闯入私人领地, Trespass

侵入者/侵犯者, Trespasser

亲权, Parental rights

亲属, Relative(s)

亲属/相对的, Relative

亲子时间, Parenting time

亲子时间稽查员, Parenting time expeditors

青少年/13岁到19岁的年轻人, Teenager

青少年/青春期的, Adolescent

青少年的/幼稚的, Juvenile

青少年犯罪, Juvenile delinquency

轻薄的/轻率的, Frivolous

轻视/蔑视, Contempt

轻松/缓解, Relief

轻罪, Petty offense

轻罪/不正当的行为, Misdemeanor

轻罪/过失, Petty misdemeanor

清醒的/稳重的, Sober

情景/地点/景色, Scene

情况/案例, Case

请求/要求, Ask for

请求/要求, Request

请求/要求, Request

请求变更, Change of plea

请求权/索赔, Claim

请愿人/上诉人/离婚案原告, Petitioner

请愿书/诉状/申请, Petition

请允许我, May it please the court

囚徒, Prisoner

囚徒/被收容者, Inmate

驱逐/依法收回, Evict

驱逐/依法收回, Eviction

取消资格/要求撤换, Recuse

圈套/俘获, Entrapment

权力/当局/专家, Authority

权利/右, Right

权利告诫, Advisement of rights

权益净额, Net equity

全部的/总体来说, Overall

全面生效/全力, Full force

全职/全日制, Full time

缺席判决, Default judgment

确定无罪/免除责任, Exonerate

确认/肯定, Affirm

确信/定罪, Conviction

然而/但是, Whereas

扰乱治安, Disturbing the peace

扰乱治安行为, Disorderly conduct

人力资源, Human resources

人身保护令, Habeas corpus

人身管束, Physical custody

人身伤害, Personal injury

人员/员工/人事部门, Personnel

仁慈/温和, Clemency

认罪, Plea of Guilty

认罪/无罪申诉, Plead guilty/not guilty

认罪谈判, Plea negotiations

认罪协议, Plea agreement

任命/指定, Appoint

任性的/故意的, Willful

日程/安排, Schedule

日历/日程表, Calendar

日托, Daycare

入店行窃, Shoplifting

入监通知书, Notice of entry

软禁于家中, House arrest

骚扰, Harass

骚扰/烦恼, Harassment

骚扰令, Harassment Order

杀人, Homicide

杀人凶器, Murder weapon

筛选/选拔/遮蔽, Screening

善意, Good faith

膳宿（在残疾的情况下）, Accommodation (in case of disability)

赡养费（离婚后丈夫给妻子的）, Alimony

赡养费（离婚后丈夫给妻子的）, Spousal maintenance

赡养判令, Maintenance order

伤害/损害, Injure

伤痕/瘀青, Bruise

商谈/授予, Confer

商业方式, Business like manner

上述的, Above-named

上述的, Aforesaid

上诉/吸引力/诉请, Appeal

上诉/吸引力/诉请, Appeal

上诉法院, Appellate Court

上诉人/上诉的, Appellant

上诉人/上诉的, Appellant

少管所, Juvenile hall

少年法庭, Juvenile court

社会保险号, Social Security Number

社区法庭, Community Court

社区服务, Community service

射击/开枪/拍照, Shoot

涉嫌发誓, Suspected of Swear

赦免/原谅, Pardon

赦免委员会, Board of Pardons

申请, Apply for

申请/存档, Filed

申请/应用, Application

申请费, Application fee

申请费, Filing fee

申请人, Applicant

申诉/答辩/辩护, Plead

身体虐待, Physical abuse

身体伤害, Bodily harm

审查/审核/复习, Review

审理案件, Hear a case

审判, Bring to trial

审判地/会场/犯罪地点, Venue

审判前的, Pretrial

审前动议, Pre-trial motion

审前犯罪, Pretrial offense

审前会议, Pre-trial conference

审讯/试验, Trial

生活费, Living expenses

生前遗嘱, Living Will

声称的/不可靠的, Alleged

失业/失业人数, Unemployment

失业补偿金, Unemployment compensation

失职/行为不当, Malpractice

时效, Statute of limitations

实施/强制执行, Enforce

食肉动物, Predator

使（排队）, Line-up

使...熄灭/用...涂掉, Blacken out

使无效, Invalidate

使误解/把...带错路, Misleading

使用暴力威胁的严重罪行, Assault, aggravated

市法院, Municipal court

市检察长, City Attorney

事情/物质/要紧, Matter

事实, Fact

事实上, In fact

事实性争论, Factual contention

事实依据, Factual basis

适当的注意/适当的通知, Proper notice

适格年龄, Suitable age

适用于, Apply to

室/会所, Chambers

室友, Roommate

释放条件, Conditions of release

誓言/誓约, Oath

收回/重新占有, Repossession

收缴欠款的代理公司, Collection agency

收缴欠款服务, Collection services

收款员, Collector

收取利息, Interest charging

收入/收益, Income

收入分配指南, Income share guidelines

收入收回, Revenue recapture

收押不得保释, Held without bail

收养/采纳, Adoption

收养/采纳/批准, Adopt

手铐和脚镣, Handcuffs and leg-irons

守法的, Law-abiding

首字母, Initials

寿险保单, Life insurance policy

受到侵犯的/（因受伤害）愤愤不平的, Aggrieved

受到召唤的, Summoned

受供养人, Dependent

受辱/被欺负, Hazing

受伤处/损害, Injury

受审, Go to trial

受损的, Impaired

授权/委任状, Authorization

授权令，逮捕, Warrant, arrest

授权令，搜查, Warrant, search

授权令/证明是正当的, Warrant

授权书, Power of attorney

授予/给予/奖金, Award

书/账目/预约, Book

书记的/事务上的, Clerical

书记员, Court clerk

疏忽, Carelessness

疏忽/渎职, Negligence

疏忽/监管, Oversight

疏忽驾驶, Careless driving

署名者/在下面签字的, Undersigned

数量/总额, Amount

双方商定, Mutually-agreed upon

税/征税, Tax

税收抵消, Tax offset

司法的/法院的/法官的, Judiciary

司法的/公正的, Judicial

司法权/管辖权, Jurisdiction

司法辖区, Judicial District

私人医疗保险, Private health care coverage

死囚区, Death Row

死刑, Capital punishment

死刑, Death penalty

死罪, Capital offense, crime

四分之一/一个季度/一刻钟, Quarter

送达回执, Admission of Service

送达证明书, Affidavit of Service

搜查/调查, Search

搜查令, Search warrant

搜查与扣押, Search and Seizure

诉讼, Litigate

诉讼/控诉, Lawsuit

诉讼/起诉, Litigation

诉讼/请求/适合/满足, Suit

诉讼案件, Case of action

诉讼当事人/诉讼的, Litigant

诉讼文件移送命令, Certiorari

诉状/恳求, Pleadings

速度限制, Speed limit

随身用品/已婚妇女的私人财产, Paraphernalia

损失/失败, Loss

所得税, Income Tax

所得税退税, Income tax refund

所有者权益, Ownership interest

探视权, Visitation rights

逃学/玩忽职守, Truancy

逃走/飞逝, Flee

特权/优惠, Privilege

特赦, Pardon extraordinary

疼痛和痛苦, Pain and suffering

提出无罪抗辩, Plea of Innocence

提起法律诉讼, Initiate legal proceedings

提起诉讼, Bring an action

提起诉讼, File suit

提问和回答, Asked and answered

提讯/传讯/责难, Arraignment

题目/称号/权益, Title

天使粉, Angel dust

挑战/质疑, Challenge

挑战/质疑, Challenge

条/项目/物品, Item

条件/情况, Conditions

条款和条件, Terms and conditions

调查/结果/（陪审团的）裁决, Finding

调度员/调度器, Dispatcher

调度中心, Dispatch center

调解/仲裁, Mediation

调解法庭, Conciliation Court

调解服务, Mediation services

调解人/中介人, Mediator

调整/适应, Adjustment

听从, Submitted

听从/提交, Submit

听到/审讯/听证会, Hearing

听证官, Hearing officer

听证会，有争议的, Hearing, contested

庭前会议, Bench conference

庭外和解, Out-of-court settlement

停止, Cease and desist

停止/终止, Terminate

停止对该案提出证据, Rest the case

通常/平常, Usually

通道/接近, Access

通告, Public notice/warning

通勤/减刑, Commute

通知者/告密者, Informant

同案被告, Co-defendant

同伴, Companion

同意/批准, Approval

同意/一致, Agree

同意/准许, Consent

偷窃/失窃, Theft

头部内部受伤, Internal head injury

投诉/控告/起诉状, Complaint

投资/授予, Invest

投资/投资额, Investment

图像识别, Picture identification

涂掉/省略, Expungement

推测/怀疑/可疑的/嫌疑犯, Suspect

推迟, Postponement

推迟/服从, Defer

推迟/延期, Postpone

推迟宣判, Deferred sentence

退出（比赛或竞选）/（从某职位上）退下, Stand down

退款, Refund

退伍年金, Veteran's benefits

退休金, Retirement benefits

拖吊厂, Impound lot

拖欠款项/待做的工作, Arrears

外国的/陌生的, Alien

外在的/非本质的, Extrinsic

完好无缺的, Intact

晚期病症, Terminal illness

晚些时候, Later date

危害/受到危害, Endangerment

危及/危害, Endanger

威慑的/制止的, Deterrent

威胁/恐吓, Threat

威胁/预示, Threaten

为…主持宣誓仪式, Administer the oath to…

为自己辩护, Enter a plea

违法/违反, Infraction

违反/妨碍, Violation

违反/侵犯/妨碍, Violate

违规局, Violations bureau

违约/默认, Default

违者受…的处罚, Under penalty of

维护正义, Interest of justice

伪造/伪造罪/赝品, Forgery

伪证（罪）, Perjury

伪证罪, Penalty of perjury

委员会/佣金, Commission

猥亵儿童, Child molestation

卫生保健, Health care

未偿还的, Unreimbursed

未偿清的债务, Outstanding debts

未付的/未缴纳的, Unpaid

未能/失败, Failure to

未能出庭, Failure to appear

未能作出裁定的陪审团, Hung jury

未投保险的, Uninsured

位置/场所, Location

文件编号, File number

文件费, File charges

文件归档/锉, Filing

问题/发行/颁布, Issue

问题/发行/颁布, Issue

无节制的/肆无忌惮的, Wanton

无可挽回的婚姻破裂, Irretrievable breakdown of the marriage

无利害关系的第三方, Disinterested Third Party

无偏见/不受损害, Without prejudice

无期徒刑, Life imprisonment

无期徒刑, Life sentence

无损害驳回起诉(可以再诉), Dismiss without prejudice

无条件释放, Unconditional release

无效审判/误判, Mistrial

无资格的/不适当的, Ineligible

无罪申诉（刑事诉讼中, 被告不认罪但又放弃申辩）, Nolo contendere

无罪申诉, Plea of not-guilty

无罪推定, Presumption of innocence

武器，隐藏的, Weapon, concealed

武器，致命的, Weapon, deadly

武器/兵器, Weapon

武装部队, Armed forces

物体/目的/反对, Object

物证, Material evidence

物主/所有人, Owner

西班牙的/西班牙语的/西班牙人的, Hispanic

行动/起诉/作用, Action

行为/契约, Deed

行为不捡/管理或处理不当, Misconduct

吸入/招收/入口, Intake

袭击/抨击, Assault

洗钱, Money laundering

下落/所在之处, Whereabouts

现场清醒测试, Field sobriety Test

现有秩序, Existing order

现值, Present value

限时产权, Time share

限制/抑制, Restraints

宪法权利, Constitutional right

相信/信念, Belief

响应或反对, Respond or object

小额索偿, Small Claims

小额索偿法院, Small claims court

小陪审团, Petit Jury

小偷小摸, Petty theft

小学入学年龄, Elementary school age

协议/一致, Agreement

协议/一致, Agreement

携带武器的权利, Right to bear arms

心理健康, Mental health

新闻报道/涵盖范围, Coverage

信息/通知, Information

刑事司法权益相关者, Criminal justice stakeholders

形式/表格/产生, Form

性犯罪, Sexual offense

性格/部署, Disposition

性虐待, Sexual abuse

性侵犯, Sexual assault

性侵犯, Sexual Assault

性侵犯者, Sexual predator

性罪犯, Sexual offender

性罪犯治疗, Sexual offender treatment

姓氏, Last name

休假/公休, Furlough

休庭, Court is adjourned

休庭/延期, Adjourn

休庭期间/延期, Adjournment

休息/打破, Break

修订/改进, Amend

修订/改进/修正案, Amendment

修改/修改, Modify/modification

修改后的信息, Amended information

许可证/准许, License

蓄意地/任性故意地, Willfully

蓄意行为, Willful act

蓄意作案, Loitering with intent

宣布不合格/取消资格, Recusal

宣告无罪, Acquit

宣告无罪, Acquittal

宣过誓, Under oath

宣判, Pronounce sentence

宣判/句子, Sentence

宣判/句子, Sentence

宣誓, Take an oath

宣誓书, Affidavit

宣誓作证, Depose

学龄前儿童, Preschooler

学校/学业, School

血醇水平, Blood alcohol level

血液酒精测试, Blood alcohol test

询问，直接的, Examination, direct

训示权, Right of allocution

延期, Deferment

延期/延长/扩大, Extension

延伸/提供, Extend

严重的轻罪, Gross misdemeanor

言论自由, Freedom of speech

验尸官, Coroner

养成/培育, Nurturance/Nurturing

养老金/抚恤金, Pension

药物滥用, Drug abuse

一般援助, General Assistance

一方/当事人/政党, Party

一级, First degree

一罪两罚, Double jeopardy

医疗事故, Medical malpractice

医疗事故保险, Malpractice insurance

医疗援助, Medical Assistance

医疗支持, Medical support

依赖/信赖, Dependence

依赖于, Depending on

移交, Set over

移居/移民, Immigration

移民身份/入境身份, Immigration status

移送管辖, Change of venue

遗弃/放纵, Abandonment

遗嘱, Will

遗嘱查验/遗嘱查讫证, Probate

已付款的, Paid

已婚的/婚姻的, Married

已取得的利息, Interest earned

以…的身份行事, Acting in the capacity of

以贫民的身份免付诉讼费, In forma pauperis

意味着/暗示, Implicate

因此/特此, Hereby

因果关系, Causation

银行对账单, Bank statement

银行税, Bank levy

引渡逃犯, Extradition

引用/传票, Citation

引用/传讯, Cite

引诱/诱使, Entice

隐匿证据, Suppress evidence

隐私, Privacy

印刷/出版, Print

婴儿/初期的, Infant

应...的请求, At the request of

应付款项, Payables

应有的注意/尽职调查, Due diligence

拥护/支持/鼓吹, Advocacy

拥护/支持/鼓吹, Advocate

永久性居民, Permanent resident

用致命武器袭击, Assault with a deadly weapon

优点/好处, Advantage

优点/价值/值得, Merit

优先的/在前的, Priors

由陪审团进行的审讯, Jury trial

有关的/切题的, Relevant

有继父（或继母）的家庭, Step-Family

有理由/无理由, Ground/not grounds for

有偏见/有损, With prejudice

有伤风化的暴露, Indecent exposure

有损害驳回起诉(不可以再诉), Dismiss with prejudice

有限的例外, Limited exception

有限责任, Limited liability

有限责任公司, Limited liability corporation

有诱导性的提问, Leading question

有争议的案件, Contested case

有正当理由的反对, Challenge for cause

有追溯力的, Retroactive

有资格的, Qualified

有罪答辩, Guilty plea

诱惑/吸引, Lure

诱人/诱惑, Enticement

娱乐/招待, Entertain

预谋/恶意, Malice

预审程序, Preliminary hearing

预先安排的, Scheduled

预约, Booking

预约号, Booking number

原告, Complainant

原告, Plaintiff

原始的/原版的/原创的, Original

月付款额, Monthly payment

运动/示意/动议, Motion

再次直接询问, Redirect examination

再犯, Repeat violation

在进行中, Under way

在先的/在前的, Preceding

暂时的/临时的, Temporary

暂停/休庭, Recess

暂准监外工作, Work furlough

赞同/背书于, Endorse

责任/倾向/不利因素, Liability

责任/税, Duty

诈骗, Defraud

摘要/抽象的/提取, Abstract

债权人, Creditor

债权人, Debt-holder

债权人, Obligee

债务/义务, Debt

债务人, Debtor

债务人, Obligor

占有判决, Judgment for possession

长期的, Long-term

长期放置的设施, Long-term placement facility

招供/认错, Confession

招致/引起, Incur

召唤/召集/传票, Summon

照料、保管和控制, Care, custody and control

肇事后逃逸, Hit-and-run

折扣/低估/不信, Discount

真实和正确的, True and correct

争端/质疑, Dispute

争夺/辩驳, Contest

征税/税款, Levy

征信社, Credit Bureau

正当的/有根据的, Well grounded

正义/司法, Justice

证词/见证, Testimony

证据，辩方的, Exhibit, defense's

证据，间接的, Evidence, circumstantial

证据，直接的, Evidence, direct

证据/迹象, Evidence

证据/提出证据/展出, Exhibit

证据/证明, Proof

证据不足不能定罪/疑罪从无/无罪推定, Innocent until proven guilty

证据规则, Rules of Evidence

证据排除规则, Exclusionary rule

证据听证会, Evidentiary hearing

证据优势, Preponderance of evidence

证明/结果是, Prove

证明/结果是, Proving

证明力, Weight of evidence

证明有罪/宣判有罪, Convict

证人, 辩方, Witness, defense

证人, 恶意, Witness, hostile

证人，控方, Witness, prosecution

证人，能提供实质性证据的, Witness, material

证人, 专家, Witness, expert

证人/提出口供者, Deponent

证人/证言/目击, Witness

证人席, Witness stand

证实/发证书给, Certify

证实为成年人, Certify as an adult

证言/宣誓作证, Deposition

政府援助, Public assistance

政府中心, Government Center

支持/拥护, Support

支持性文件, Supporting documents

支票抬头, Payable to

执法机构, Law enforcement agencies

执法人员, Law enforcement officer

执行令状, Writ of execution

执照/认可, Certificate

直接证据, Direct evidence

职员, Clerk

指导方针/准则, Guidelines

指控, Accusation

指控, Accuse

指控/管理/费用, Charge

指控/管理/费用, Charge

指南/教程/辅导的, Tutorial

指纹, Finger print

指纹识别, Fingerprinting

致命的武器, Deadly weapon

智力缺陷, Mental retardation

中间名, Middle name

终身寿险, Whole life insurance

终身职位/任期, Tenure

终生监禁, Life in prison

仲裁/公断, Arbitration

重大问题, Significant issue

重要的/有意义的, Significant

重罪, Felony

重罪犯, Felon

州地方法院, District Court

逐字的, Verbatim

主要财产, Principal assets

主要照料者, Primary care giver

主张/辩论, Argue

助学贷款, Student loan

住处/居住, Residence

住房, Housing

注意/观察/通知, Notice

抓住/没收, Seize

专横的罢工或挑战, Peremptory strike or challenge

专家证人, Expert witness

专员/委员, Commissioner

装饰/出庭传票/扣押债权的通知, Garnishment

装饰/传讯, Garnish

咨询服务, Counseling service

资产/优点, Assets

滋扰誓言, Nuisance Oath

子女抚养费, Child Support

自雇, Self-employment

自己的/特有的, Own

自卫/正当防卫, Self-defense

自我担保, Own recognizance

自由裁量权的滥用, Abuse of discretion

自愿地/自动地, Voluntarily

自证其罪, Self-incrimination

自尊, Self-worth

综合人寿保险, Universal life insurance

总检察长/司法部长, Attorney General

总检察长办公室, Attorney General's Office

总结/总和, Summation

纵火/纵火罪, Arson

纵火犯, Arsonist

租赁协议, Rental agreement

租用/雇用, Hire

租约/出租/租得, Lease

足够的/充分的, Sufficient

阻止/排除, Precluding

最低支付额, Minimum payment

最高法院, Supreme Court

最高法院的陪审法官, Associate justice of the Supreme Court

最高法院的陪审法官/助理法官, Associate justice

最后期限, Deadline

最后为人所知的地址, Last known address

罪犯/冒犯者, Offender

遵从/服从, Comply

遵守/履行, Abide by

作出裁决, Return a verdict

作为监护人/非监护人的父母, Custodial/Non-Custodial Parent

作为监护人的父母, Custodial parent

作证/证明, Testify

做出判令, Enter an order

ABOUT THE AUTHOR

For more than 25 years, José Luis Leyva has been a translator and interpreter in various technical areas. His vast experience in bilingualism has allowed him to interpret for Presidents, Latin American and US governors, ambassadors, CEO's, judges, prosecutors, forensic experts and healthcare professionals. He is also the author of other books, including technical terminology books of the ***Essential Technical Terminology*** series.

45235961R00090

Made in the USA
Lexington, KY
21 September 2015